# Mind's Eye Unveiled

## The Gestalt Path to Problem-Solving Insight

**Freudian Trips**

# Copyright Page



Published by Omniterra Media Inc

First Edition

Visit the author's website at www.freudiantrips.com

# Disclaimer

The views and opinions expressed in this book are those of the author(s) and do not necessarily reflect the official policy or position of any other agency, organization, employer, or company. The contents of this book are for informational and educational purposes only and are not intended to serve as professional advice, diagnosis, or treatment.

The information provided in this book is believed to be accurate and reliable as of the date of publication. However, it may include some errors or inaccuracies, and no warranty or guarantee is provided regarding the accuracy, timeliness, or applicability of the content.

Readers are encouraged to consult with professional philosophers, educators, or other qualified professionals where appropriate for personalized advice. The author(s) and publisher shall not be liable for any loss, damage, or harm caused or alleged to be caused, directly or indirectly, by the information or ideas contained, suggested, or referenced in this book.

By reading this book, the reader acknowledges and agrees that they are solely responsible for how they interpret and apply the information contained herein.

This book may also include references to other works, studies, and sources. These references are provided for further reading and exploration and do not imply endorsement or validation of the specific theories, viewpoints, or interpretations presented in those works.

# Introduction - The Gestalt Gateway to Insightful Problem-Solving

## Overview of Gestalt Theory

Imagine looking at a scattered puzzle. At first, all you see are fragmented pieces. But when you start piecing them together, a clear picture emerges. This is the essence of Gestalt Theory, a psychological approach that teaches us to see the 'whole' rather than just the 'parts.' Developed in the early 20th century, Gestalt Theory began as a way to understand how we perceive things visually. It suggests that our brains are wired to organize information into meaningful wholes. Think of the famous saying, "The whole is greater than the sum of its parts." That's Gestalt Theory in a nutshell.

## The Importance of Insight in Problem-Solving

Have you ever been stuck on a problem, only to have the solution suddenly come to you in a flash of insight? That "Aha!" moment is what Gestalt Theory is all about. Insight is like a lightbulb turning on in your mind, illuminating the path to a solution. It's different from the step-by-step logical thinking we're often taught. Instead of painstakingly analyzing every detail, insight allows you to leap to a solution intuitively and creatively. It's like seeing the puzzle picture without having to fit every piece together.

## The Relevance of Gestalt Principles in Contemporary Problem-Solving

In today's fast-paced, complex world, the ability to solve problems through insight is more valuable than ever. We are constantly bombarded with information, making it tough to see the 'big picture.' Gestalt Theory offers a fresh perspective. It encourages us to step back and view problems holistically, looking for patterns and connections that might not be immediately obvious. This approach is incredibly useful in fields ranging from business to education, design, and technology. By applying Gestalt principles, we can become better problem-solvers, able to navigate the complexities of modern life with greater ease and creativity.

In summary, Gestalt Theory opens up a world where understanding the whole can lead to innovative solutions, transforming the way we tackle problems in our daily lives. This chapter sets the stage for exploring how we can all harness the power of insight to solve problems more effectively and creatively.

# Chapter 1: Foundations of Gestalt Theory

## The Roots of Gestalt Psychology

Let's take a step back in time to the early 20th century, a period buzzing with new ideas in psychology. This was when Gestalt Theory began. It emerged as a reaction against the prevalent thinking of the time, which broke down human perception into tiny parts. The founders of Gestalt Theory believed this approach missed the bigger picture - literally. They argued that our minds naturally prefer to see things as complete wholes, not just as a collection of parts.

## Pioneers of Gestalt Psychology

Three psychologists stand at the forefront of this revolutionary idea: Max Wertheimer, Wolfgang Köhler, and Kurt Koffka. These three thinkers were like the rockstars of psychology in their time. They each brought unique insights and experiments to the table, which collectively shaped the Gestalt movement.

Max Wertheimer was the one who kick-started it all. He was intrigued by the way we perceive motion and conducted experiments that led to major breakthroughs in understanding perception.

Wolfgang Köhler conducted famous experiments with animals, showing that they could solve problems not just by trial and error but through sudden understanding or insight - a key Gestalt concept.

Kurt Koffka helped spread Gestalt ideas far and wide. He was particularly interested in applying these concepts to the development of children's perceptions and thinking.

**Basic Principles of Gestalt Psychology**

Now, let's unpack the core ideas of Gestalt Theory. These principles are surprisingly simple yet profound in understanding how we perceive the world:

**The Whole is Different from the Sum of Its Parts:** This is the cornerstone of Gestalt Theory. It means that when we look at something, our brain prefers to see the complete form first, rather than just an assembly of its components.

**Figure-Ground Relationship:** Think of a picture where an image pops out against a background. Our perception naturally divides what we see into the 'figure' (the main element) and the 'ground' (the backdrop). This helps us make sense of complex visuals.

**Proximity and Similarity:** Objects that are close together or similar in appearance tend to be perceived as part of the same group.

**Closure:** Our brains like to 'fill in the gaps.' If we see a broken circle, we tend to mentally complete it. This principle shows our tendency to see complete, familiar patterns even when parts are missing.

**Continuity:** We perceive smooth, continuous patterns rather than disjointed ones. For example, a series of dots aligned can be seen as a line or wave, creating a sense of continuity.

**Simplicity:** Gestalt psychology suggests that we naturally prefer simple, stable, and consistent shapes and forms.

These principles guide our understanding of how the mind interprets visual information, but their influence goes beyond just perception. They play a crucial role in how we think, learn, and solve problems.

In this chapter, we've explored the foundations of a theory that revolutionized psychology. As we move forward, we'll see how these ideas help unlock the mysteries of the human mind and its problem-solving prowess.

# Chapter 2: The Insight Phenomenon

**Exploring Insight in Problem-Solving**

Have you ever been stumped by a problem, only to have the answer suddenly pop into your head? This experience, often accompanied by a mental exclamation of "Aha!" is what psychologists refer to as 'insight.' Insight is a bit like a mental magic trick, where the solution to a problem appears unexpectedly, without the step-by-step reasoning we usually use. It's an exciting, mysterious, and deeply human experience.

**The "Aha!" Moment: Understanding Sudden Realizations**

The "Aha!" moment is the hallmark of insight. It's that instant when the clouds of confusion clear, and you see the solution clearly. It's as if your brain has been working backstage, piecing together the puzzle without you consciously knowing it. Then, in a burst of revelation, the answer appears. This moment is not just psychologically satisfying; it's also a fascinating window into the way our minds work. It shows us that our brains are capable of processing information and solving problems in ways that we are not always consciously aware of.

These moments of insight are more than just mental shortcuts. They are often the birthplace of creative and innovative solutions. Think about famous inventors or scientists who had sudden breakthroughs; their insights have sometimes changed the world.

## Insight vs. Analytical Problem-Solving

To understand insight better, let's compare it with its more methodical cousin, analytical problem-solving. Analytical problem-solving is the systematic, logical approach we're all familiar with. It's like following a recipe step by step. You understand each step, and you can see how one leads to the next. This approach is reliable, but it can be slow and often requires a lot of mental energy.

Insight, on the other hand, is like taking a shortcut through the woods that you didn't know existed. It's faster and can be more efficient, but it's also unpredictable. You can't always force an insight to happen, and sometimes the path it takes can be a bit mysterious.

One isn't necessarily better than the other. In fact, the best problem solvers are those who can use both approaches, switching between analytical thinking and insight as needed. Sometimes you need the thoroughness and certainty of analysis, and other times, especially when facing new or particularly complex problems, insight can provide the breakthrough you need.

In summary, insight in problem-solving is a sudden and often unexpected understanding of a problem. It contrasts with the step-by-step process of analytical problem-solving by offering a quicker, more intuitive path to solutions. Understanding and harnessing this phenomenon can transform the way we approach challenges, both big and small, in our daily lives. As we move through this book, we'll explore ways to cultivate and encourage these "Aha!" moments, unlocking our potential for creative and efficient problem-solving.

# Chapter 3: Gestalt Principles Applied to Problem-Solving

**Harnessing Proximity, Similarity, and Closure in Problem-Solving**

Let's dive into how some key Gestalt principles – proximity, similarity, and closure – can be applied to problem-solving. These principles might sound technical, but they're really about the everyday ways we make sense of the world.

**Proximity:** This principle tells us that things which are close together are seen as related. In problem-solving, this means if you group related parts of a problem together, it can make the problem easier to understand and solve. For instance, if you're trying to organize your weekly tasks, grouping them by context – work, home, errands – can make your to-do list less overwhelming.

**Similarity:** According to this principle, we see things that look similar as being part of the same group. This can help in problem-solving by allowing us to classify and organize information. Imagine you're sorting a pile of clothes. Grouping them by color or type (like all T-shirts together) makes the task smoother.

**Closure:** This principle is about our mind's ability to 'fill in the gaps' and see complete pictures even when parts are missing. In problem-solving, this means we can often see the solution to a problem as a 'whole' even when we don't have all the information. It's like solving a jigsaw puzzle – you can often guess what the missing pieces might look like based on the pieces you have.

## The Role of Perception in Understanding Problems

Perception is not just about how we see things with our eyes; it's also about how we understand and interpret the world around us. When it comes to problem-solving, how we perceive the problem can often define how we solve it. For example, if you see a problem as a threat, you might approach it with anxiety and stress. But if you see it as a challenge, your approach can be more creative and positive. The Gestalt principles remind us to step back and look at the problem in a new light. Sometimes, simply changing our perspective can make a problem seem more manageable.

## Breaking Down Complexity: Gestalt Approach to Simplification

Life's problems can often feel complex and overwhelming. The Gestalt approach to simplification is about breaking down these complex problems into simpler, more manageable parts. It encourages us to look for patterns, connections, and the 'big picture.' This doesn't mean ignoring the details but rather understanding how these details fit into a larger context.

A practical example could be budgeting. Instead of getting bogged down by every single expense, you can group expenses into categories (like food, utilities, entertainment). This not only simplifies the process but also gives you a clearer picture of your spending habits.

In conclusion, applying Gestalt principles to problem-solving is about seeing problems in a new way. It's about grouping related elements, recognizing patterns, and understanding the bigger picture. By simplifying complexity and changing our perspective, we can approach problems more effectively and creatively. This chapter has shown that the way we see problems can profoundly influence the way we solve them.

# Chapter 4: Barriers to Insight

## Understanding Mental Set and Functional Fixedness

First, let's explore two common barriers to insight: mental set and functional fixedness. These might sound like complex terms, but they're actually simple concepts that describe how our usual way of thinking can get in the way of finding new solutions.

**Mental Set:** This is when we stick to solutions that have worked in the past, even when they might not be the best choice for a current problem. It's like always using the same recipe for soup without considering other ingredients that might make it taste better. Our previous experiences can limit our ability to see alternative solutions.

**Functional Fixedness:** This term describes our tendency to see objects and tools only in their traditional roles. For example, if you only think of a hammer as a tool to drive nails, you might not consider using it as a paperweight. This kind of fixed thinking can prevent us from seeing creative solutions to problems.

## Overcoming Bias and Assumptions

Biases and assumptions are like invisible filters through which we see the world. They can color our judgment and decision-making, often without us even realizing it.

**Biases:** These are preconceived notions or tendencies to think in a certain way. For instance, if you believe that a task is too hard, you might not even try to find a solution, assuming it's out of reach.

**Assumptions:** These are things we take for granted or believe to be true without question. For example, if you assume you need a certain tool to fix something, you might not consider alternative methods that could work just as well or even better.

Recognizing and challenging our biases and assumptions is crucial for clear thinking and effective problem-solving. It opens our minds to new possibilities and perspectives.

## Strategies for Breaking Mental Blocks

**So, how do we break through these barriers to insight? Here are some strategies:**

**Change Your Routine:** Sometimes, simply changing your environment or routine can spark new ideas. If you're stuck, try working in a different location or at a different time.

**Question Everything:** Challenge your assumptions by asking questions like, "What if this isn't true?" or "Is there another way to look at this?"

**Brainstorming:** This is a technique where you allow yourself to come up with as many ideas as possible, no matter how silly they might seem. It helps to break free from conventional thinking patterns.

**Take Breaks:** Sometimes, stepping away from a problem can help clear your mind. When you come back, you might see things from a fresh perspective.

**Seek Different Perspectives:** Talk to people with different backgrounds or expertise. They might see the problem in a way you hadn't considered.

**Try Reverse Thinking:** Instead of thinking about how to solve the problem, think about how you could cause or worsen it. This reverse approach can sometimes reveal insights into solving it.

In this chapter, we've looked at common barriers to insight and how to overcome them. By understanding and addressing these barriers, we can unlock our full problem-solving potential, leading to more creative and effective solutions in our personal and professional lives.

# Chapter 5: Cultivating Insight in Everyday Life

**Techniques for Enhancing Insightful Thinking**

Developing the ability to have insights is like nurturing a garden; it requires care, patience, and the right environment. Here are some techniques to cultivate insightful thinking in your everyday life:

**Embrace Curiosity:** Stay curious about everything. Like a child, ask questions about the world around you. Curiosity opens the door to new ideas and perspectives, which are the seeds of insight.

**Keep a Journal:** Writing down your thoughts, experiences, and reflections can help clarify your thinking. It also allows you to revisit old ideas, which might spark new insights.

**Play with Problems:** Approach problems playfully, like puzzles to be solved. This light-hearted approach can reduce pressure, making it easier for insights to surface.

**Diversify Your Experiences:** Expose yourself to different environments, cultures, and fields of knowledge. The more diverse your experiences, the broader your thinking, and the greater your potential for insights.

**Rest and Relaxation:** Never underestimate the power of a good night's sleep or a relaxing break. Often, insights come when we're not actively trying to solve a problem.

## Mindfulness and Openness to Experience

Mindfulness and openness are crucial for insightful thinking. They involve being present in the moment and receptive to new experiences and ideas.

**Practice Mindfulness:** This means paying full attention to whatever you're doing, whether it's eating, walking, or listening. Mindfulness helps clear mental clutter, making room for new insights.

**Be Open to New Experiences:** Embrace new ideas, even if they seem unusual or outside your comfort zone. Openness enhances your ability to make unexpected connections, a key component of insight.

## Creative Exercises Based on Gestalt Principles

Gestalt principles aren't just theories; they can be applied through simple, creative exercises that enhance your ability to see things in new ways.

**Reframe the Problem:** Sometimes, just stating a problem differently can open up new solutions. Try expressing your problem in various ways to see it from new angles.

**Visualization:** Imagine the problem and its potential solutions visually. How do the pieces fit together? Can you see a pattern or a whole image?

**Role Play:** Pretend you are someone else approaching your problem. How would a scientist, an artist, or a child view it?

**Connect the Unconnected:** Take two unrelated ideas and try to find connections between them. This exercise stretches your creative muscles and can lead to surprising insights.

**Use Metaphors:** Describe your problem using a metaphor. For example, if your problem is a 'tangled mess,' what tools would you use to 'untangle' it? This approach can provide new perspectives.

By integrating these techniques and exercises into your daily life, you can nurture your ability to think insightfully. Insightful thinking is not just about sudden eureka moments; it's a skill that can be developed and refined, enhancing your creativity, problem-solving abilities, and overall enjoyment of life.

# Chapter 6: Gestalt in Group Problem-Solving

## Group Dynamics and Collective Insight

Solving problems in a group can be like orchestrating a symphony – every member has a unique part to play, and when harmonized, they create something greater than the sum of their parts. This is where Gestalt principles shine, offering valuable insights into group dynamics.

**The Power of the Group:** Just as Gestalt psychology emphasizes the whole over individual parts, in group problem-solving, the collective wisdom of the group often leads to more comprehensive and creative solutions than any single member could achieve alone.

**Diverse Perspectives:** Each group member brings their own experiences and viewpoints, offering a richer understanding of the problem. This diversity can lead to a more holistic and innovative solution, as different pieces of the puzzle come together.

## Facilitating Insightful Collaboration

**Creating an environment that fosters insightful collaboration is key. Here are some ways to encourage this:**

**Open Communication:** Encourage open and respectful dialogue. Every member should feel comfortable sharing their ideas, no matter how unconventional.

**Active Listening:** Teach group members the value of listening to understand, not just to respond. This can lead to deeper insights and more cohesive solutions.

**Encourage Diverse Thinking:** Welcome different viewpoints and approaches. Sometimes, the most unexpected idea can lead to a breakthrough.

**Build on Ideas:** Encourage members to build on each other's ideas. This collaborative effort can evolve an initial idea into a fully-formed solution.

**Designate Roles Flexibly:** While structure is important, allow flexibility in roles so members can contribute where they feel most inspired.

## Hypothetical Case Studies: Successful Group Problem-Solving

Let's look at some examples where groups have successfully applied these principles:

**Innovation in Technology:** Consider a tech company that brings together programmers, designers, and marketers to brainstorm a new product. The diversity of their expertise leads to a product that's not only technically sound but also user-friendly and marketable.

**Community Projects:** A community working together to solve a local issue, like organizing a recycling program. By pooling their resources, knowledge, and efforts, they achieve a sustainable and practical solution.

**Medical Research Teams:** Medical researchers often work in interdisciplinary teams. By combining knowledge from different medical fields, they can approach complex medical problems with greater depth and creativity.

In summary, applying Gestalt principles in group problem-solving can enhance the effectiveness and creativity of the solutions. By understanding and harnessing the dynamics of group interaction and encouraging an environment of diverse thinking and collaborative effort, groups can achieve remarkable insights and innovative solutions. This chapter highlights the potential of collective intelligence and the transformative power of collaborative problem-solving.

# Chapter 7: Gestalt Therapy and Personal Growth

**Exploring Gestalt Therapy Techniques**

Gestalt therapy, a form of psychotherapy, can offer intriguing ways to understand ourselves and grow. It's based on the idea that personal experience is more about perception and context rather than objective reality. Here are some key techniques used in Gestalt therapy:

**The Here and Now:** This technique focuses on what is happening at the present moment, rather than what has happened in the past or what might happen in the future. It encourages people to fully experience their current feelings, thoughts, and actions.

**Empty Chair Technique:** This involves talking to an empty chair as if another person, a part of yourself, or a certain aspect of your life is seated there. It's a way to explore different viewpoints and emotions, leading to deeper self-understanding.

**Exaggeration Exercise:** This involves exaggerating a movement or gesture repeatedly to intensify the awareness of feelings associated with it. For instance, if someone habitually shrugs their shoulders, asking them to exaggerate this movement can reveal emotions of helplessness or indifference.

## Self-awareness and Personal Insight

Gestalt therapy is deeply rooted in the concept of self-awareness. It's about understanding our own perceptions, behaviors, and feelings and recognizing how they shape our experiences.

**Mindfulness:** Similar to the principles of mindfulness, Gestalt therapy encourages being fully present and aware of one's experiences without judgment. This heightened awareness can lead to profound personal insights and a better understanding of one's behavior patterns.

**Exploring Relationships:** Gestalt therapy often explores how individuals interact with others. Understanding these dynamics can lead to insights about how one's behavior affects relationships and vice versa.

## Applying Gestalt Principles for Personal Development

The principles of Gestalt therapy can be applied for personal growth, even outside the therapy room. Here's how:

**Awareness Practice:** Regularly take time to check in with yourself. What are you feeling right now? What are your thoughts? This practice can develop self-awareness and insight.

**Responsibility for Choices:** Recognize that you are the author of your actions and decisions. Owning this responsibility can be empowering and lead to more conscious decision-making.

**Experiment with Perspectives:** Just as in the empty chair exercise, try looking at personal challenges from different perspectives. What would a friend say about your situation? How would you advise someone else in your shoes?

**Embrace Wholeness:** Remember the Gestalt principle that the whole is greater than the sum of its parts. Acknowledge all aspects of yourself – your strengths, weaknesses, successes, and failures – as integral parts of who you are.

In this chapter, we explored how Gestalt therapy can be a powerful tool for personal growth and self-discovery. By becoming more aware of our thoughts, emotions, and behaviors and understanding their impact on our lives, we can embark on a journey of self-improvement and holistic personal development.

# Chapter 8: Insightful Leadership and Management

**The Gestalt Approach to Leadership**

Leadership through the Gestalt lens involves seeing the organization as a whole – its goals, teams, and challenges – and understanding how they interconnect. This approach emphasizes holistic thinking, where a leader is not just managing people but is deeply aware of how different parts of the organization affect each other.

**Seeing the Bigger Picture:** Just as Gestalt psychology focuses on the whole rather than the sum of its parts, Gestalt leadership is about understanding how different elements of the organization contribute to its overall success.

**Empathy and Understanding:** A Gestalt leader strives to understand the experiences and perspectives of their team members. This empathetic approach helps in building stronger, more cohesive teams.

**Fostering a Culture of Insight in Organizations**

Creating an organizational culture that values and promotes insight involves more than just encouraging new ideas. It's about cultivating an environment where employees feel safe to express their thoughts, experiment, and learn from failures.

**Open Communication:** Encourage open lines of communication across all levels. This can lead to a free flow of ideas and insights throughout the organization.

**Valuing Diversity:** Diverse teams bring diverse perspectives, which are essential for insightful problem-solving. Embrace and encourage diversity in your team.

**Learning Environment:** Create a culture where learning and growth are prioritized. This includes learning from both successes and failures.

## Managing Innovation and Creativity

Innovation and creativity are at the heart of any forward-thinking organization. Managing these effectively requires a balance between structure and freedom.

**Space for Creativity:** Give employees the space and time to think creatively. This might mean setting aside time for brain-storming sessions or encouraging side projects.

**Supporting Risk-Taking:** Innovative ideas often come with risks. Create an environment where calculated risks are supported, and failure is seen as a part of the learning process.

**Resource Allocation:** Ensure that there are resources available for exploring new ideas. This could be in the form of funding, time, or access to materials and training.

**Recognition and Encouragement:** Recognize and reward creative efforts and successes. This not only motivates the team but also reinforces the value placed on innovation.

In this chapter, we've explored how the Gestalt approach to leadership and management can foster a culture of insight, innovation, and creativity in organizations. By seeing the organization as a whole, understanding the interconnectedness of its parts, and creating an environment that encourages diverse perspectives and open communication, leaders can drive their organizations towards greater success and innovation.

# Chapter 9: Gestalt in Modern Technology and AI

## AI, Machine Learning, and the Gestalt Perspective

In today's world, technology, particularly Artificial Intelligence (AI) and Machine Learning, plays a pivotal role in shaping our lives. The Gestalt perspective offers a unique lens to view these technologies.

**Holistic Data Understanding:** Just as Gestalt psychology emphasizes the whole over its parts, in AI and Machine Learning, it's essential to understand the bigger picture that data presents, not just isolated bits of information. For example, when AI analyzes health data, it's not just looking at numbers but trying to understand a person's overall health pattern.

**Pattern Recognition and Perception:** Machine Learning, a subset of AI, involves teaching computers to recognize patterns and make predictions based on them, akin to how our brains use Gestalt principles to make sense of visual information. For instance, in facial recognition technology, AI learns to identify and interpret various facial features as a whole face.

## The Future of Insightful Computing

The concept of 'insightful computing' is where AI systems not only process information but also derive insights in a way that mimics human intuition and understanding.

**Predictive Analysis:** AI can analyze vast amounts of data to predict trends and patterns. For example, it can forecast market changes or customer behavior in business.

**Creative AI:** We are on the cusp of seeing AI not just as a tool for analysis but also for creativity. AI can compose music, create art, or even write stories, opening up new realms of digital creativity.

**Personalized Experiences:** AI can tailor experiences to individual preferences, learning from user behavior. This is evident in personalized recommendations on streaming services or shopping websites.

## Ethical Considerations in AI Problem-Solving

As AI becomes more integrated into our lives, ethical considerations become increasingly important.

**Bias in AI:** AI systems are only as unbiased as the data they are trained on. If the data is biased, AI decisions will reflect that. It's crucial to ensure the data used is as unbiased and representative as possible.

**Privacy Concerns:** With AI's capability to process personal data, privacy becomes a significant concern. Balancing the benefits of AI with the right to privacy is a key challenge.

**Decision Accountability:** When AI systems make decisions, especially in critical areas like healthcare or law enforcement, it's important to have transparency and accountability in how these decisions are made.

**Future Workforce Impact:** As AI takes on more tasks, there's a concern about the impact on jobs. It's vital to consider how to transition the workforce into this new era, focusing on skills that AI can't replicate easily, like emotional intelligence and creative problem-solving.

In summary, applying Gestalt principles to modern technology and AI offers a holistic approach to data and pattern interpretation, paving the way for more intuitive and insightful computing. However, it's essential to navigate this path with a keen awareness of the ethical implications, ensuring that the advancement in AI technology aligns with societal values and benefits humanity as a whole.

# Conclusion: Embracing the Gestalt Path in Life and Problem-Solving

## The Future of Gestalt Theory in Problem-Solving

As we look towards the future, Gestalt theory continues to offer valuable insights in the realm of problem-solving. This psychological approach, which emphasizes understanding the whole rather than just its parts, has shown its relevance across various fields, from technology to education and business. In an increasingly complex world, the Gestalt approach helps us see the bigger picture, recognize patterns, and find creative solutions to the challenges we face.

The future of problem-solving lies in our ability to blend Gestalt principles with new technologies and methodologies. For instance, in fields like AI and data analysis, using Gestalt principles can lead to more intuitive and human-centric technologies. In education, these principles can help develop holistic learning approaches that encourage critical thinking and creativity.

## Integrating Insight into Daily Practices

Gestalt theory isn't just for the classroom or the therapist's office; its principles can be integrated into our daily lives. By embracing Gestalt principles, we can enhance our ability to think insightfully and solve problems more creatively. Simple practices like observing our environment more holistically, questioning our usual way of thinking, and being open to new perspectives can make a significant difference.

Incorporating these ideas into daily routines can improve personal relationships, workplace dynamics, and our overall approach to life's challenges. Whether it's in making decisions, resolving conflicts, or coming up with innovative ideas, the Gestalt approach can lead to more satisfying and effective outcomes.

## The Enduring Legacy of Gestalt Psychology

The legacy of Gestalt psychology endures because it speaks to a fundamental aspect of human nature – our innate tendency to seek patterns and meaning in the world around us. It reminds us that often, our perception of a problem or situation is as important as the objective details.

The beauty of Gestalt psychology lies in its simplicity and applicability. Its principles transcend the boundaries of psychology and find relevance in everyday life. From helping us understand how we perceive visual information to enhancing our problem-solving skills, Gestalt theory has made and continues to make a profound impact on both individual lives and society as a whole.

In conclusion, as we navigate the complexities of the modern world, the principles of Gestalt psychology offer a compass to guide us. By seeing the whole, acknowledging the interplay of parts, and embracing insight, we can approach problems with a fresh perspective and find meaningful solutions. The journey through Gestalt psychology is not just about learning a set of principles; it's about adopting a new way of seeing the world – one that values wholeness, connection, and insight.

# About Freudian Trips

Welcome to Freudian Trips, your dedicated platform for diving deep into the world of psychology. We are more than just a YouTube channel or a book publisher. We are a beacon of enlightenment, making complex psychological concepts accessible and engaging for all.

Our YouTube channel is a rich repository of psychology made simple. We take the profound and often complex ideas from the world of psychology and break them down into digestible, easy-to-understand content. From the foundational theories of Freud to the cognitive insights of Piaget, we cover a broad spectrum of psychological schools and thoughts, making psychology accessible to everyone, regardless of their background or prior knowledge.

As a book publisher, we take the same approach, transforming intricate psychological theories into comprehensible narratives. Our books are not just collections of words, but vessels of wisdom that make psychology approachable and relatable. We believe that psychology should not be confined to academic circles, but should be available to all who seek to understand the human mind and behavior.

At Freudian Trips, we believe in the power of curiosity and the pursuit of knowledge. We are here to stoke the fires of your curiosity, to guide you on your intellectual journey, and to help you navigate the fascinating world of psychology.

If you are someone who is not afraid to question, to explore, and to learn, then you are in the right place. Join us on this journey of exploration, as we make psychology easy to understand, one concept at a time.

Be sure to visit our Youtube channel at: www.freudiantrips.com/youtube

You can also visit us on the web at www.freudiantrips.com

Welcome to The Freudian Trip community. Stay curious. Stay enlightened.